D1130927

10/98

Summer

by Gail Saunders-Smith

Content Consultant:
Lisa M. Nyberg, Ph.D.
Educator, Springfield (Oregon) Public Schools

an imprint of Capstone Press

Pebble Books

Pebble Books are published by Capstone Press
818 North Willow Street, Mankato, Minnesota 56001
http://www.capstone-press.com

Library of Congress Cataloging-in-Publication Data
Saunders-Smith, Gail.
    Summer/by Gail Saunders-Smith.
        p. cm.
    Includes bibliographical references and index.
    Summary: Simple text and photographs depict the weather, plants, animals, and activities of
summer.
    ISBN 1-56065-782-0
    1. Summer—Juvenile literature. [1. Summer.] I. Title.
    QB637.6.S28 1998
    508.2—dc21   98-5041
                                                              CIP
                                                              AC

Note to Parents and Teachers

This book describes and illustrates the changes in weather, people, plants, and
animals in summer. The close picture-text matches support early readers in
understanding the text. The text offers subtle challenges with compound and
complex sentence structures. This book also introduces early readers to
expository and content-specific vocabulary. The expository vocabulary is
defined in the Words to Know section. Early readers may need assistance in
reading some of these words. Readers also may need assistance in using the
Table of Contents, Words to Know, Read More, Internet Sites, and Index/Word
List sections of the book.

Table of Contents

Summer is a season for playing and growing. Summer comes after spring and before autumn.

Some days are warm, and some are hot. Some days are humid. It is humid when the air feels hot and wet.

Sometimes storms happen. Storms bring heavy rain and strong wind. Some storms have lightning and thunder.

People have fun during summer. Many students are out of school. People play outside. They swim and skate.

Some people take vacations. Families may go camping or visit beaches. Some people go on picnics and cook outside.

Plants grow during summer. Some fruits and vegetables ripen. People pick strawberries and watermelons.

Leaves grow on trees. The leaves block the sunlight. This makes shade. Animals and people cool off in the shade.

Flowers bloom. Bees collect pollen from flowers. Pollen is a fine dust or powder that flowers make. Bees eat pollen. Hummingbirds drink nectar from flowers. Nectar is a sweet juice in flowers.

Young birds learn to fly.
They learn to find food and
care for themselves. Summer
is a season for playing
and growing.

Words to Know

autumn—the time of year between summer and winter; fall is another name for autumn

bloom—when a bud turns into a flower

fruit—a part of a plant that people eat; fruit has seeds and may taste sweet

humid—when the air feels hot and wet

lightning—a flash of bright light during a storm

nectar—a sweet juice inside some flowers

picnic—a meal that people eat outside

pollen—a fine dust or powder that flowers make; pollen helps flowers make seeds

season—one of the four parts of a year; spring, summer, autumn, and winter

shade—a cool place under a tree; the tree's leaves keep the sunlight from hitting the ground

storm—bad weather that has wind, rain, thunder, and lightning

strawberry—a sweet, red fruit that grows on a small plant

thunder—a loud boom or crash that follows lightning

vacation—a trip away from home

vegetable—a piece of a plant that people eat; vegetables usually do not taste sweet

watermelon—a sweet, juicy, pink fruit inside a round, green shell

22

Read More

Baxter, Nicola. *Summer.* Chicago: Children's Press, 1997.

Fowler, Allan. *How Do You Know It's Summer?* Chicago: Children's Press, 1992.

Gibbons, Gail. *The Reasons for Seasons.* New York: Holiday House, 1995.

Internet Sites

4 Seasons: Summer
http://www.rescol.ca/collections/agriculture/summer.html

Signs of the Season
http://www.4seasons.org.uk/projects/seasons/index.html

Weather Education-Sun
http://www.super.net.uk/Education/online/weather/sun.html

Index/Word List

Word Count: 178
Early-Intervention Level: 10

Editorial Credits
Lois Wallentine, editor; Timothy Halldin, design; Michelle L. Norstad, photo research

Photo Credits
International Stock/Bill Tucker, cover
KAC Productions/Kathy Adams Clark, 18
Richard Hamilton Smith, 4, 8, 10
Unicorn Stock Photos/Jeff Greenberg, 1; Tom, Dee Ann McCarthy, 6; Dennis MacDonald, 12; Jay Foreman, 16; John L. Ebeling, 20
Michael Worthy, 14